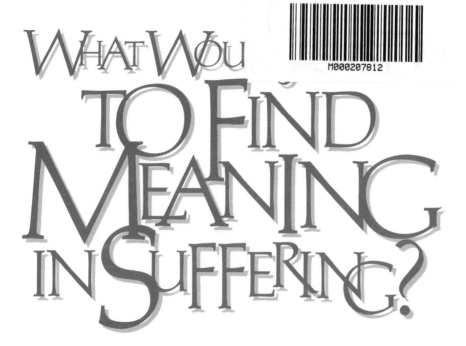

What Would It Take To Find Meaning In Suffering?

Library of Congress Catalog Number
97-78270

ISBN 0-87029-314-1

Book design by Aaron Presler

Printed in the United States of America

About the **WWJD** Books...

WWJD?—What Would Jesus Do? All of Christian belief and practice is summed up in this deceptively simple question. How can we live in love every day, as Jesus would? How can we respond with faith and hope to the problems of our lives?

As we struggle to cope with the crisis of the day—how can we do what Jesus would do?

The **WWJD Books From One Caring Place** show modern believers how to use these four little letters as a touchstone for coping with life's biggest challenges. Each lefthand page is a meditation on what Jesus would do to deal with the particular problem. Each righthand page presents a relevant Scripture passage—the Old Testament words that inspired Jesus' life, or what Jesus himself said, did, and taught in the New Testament. Drawing from the Word of God revealed in the Scriptures and in the life of Jesus, we find the strength and guidance to follow in his footsteps as we cope with our own life challenges.

Whether you read this book straight through from cover to cover, or randomly choose an inspiration for the day, may it lead you ever deeper into the Way, the Truth, and the Life of Christ. And may it remind you in the midst of every problem you face, at each juncture throughout your day: What Would Jesus Do?

Introduction

He is known as the Man of Sorrows; his cross is the universal symbol of Christianity. He insisted that his followers must take up their crosses and follow him.

From the moment the first gasp of cold air entered his infant lungs, the Son of God had to learn how to deal with pain. As a human being, he experienced physical discomfort and emotional distress, just as we do, culminating in the ultimate suffering of his passion and death. Like each of us, the human Jesus struggled to make sense of suffering.

Your suffering, whether physical or emotional, is unique. No one else feels exactly what you feel. Yet some of the same threads weave themselves through all human suffering: shattering loss, difficult questions, painful emotions, hunger for reassurance. The journey to acceptance, to peace, is long and hard.

Jesus has walked that road before you. He did not have the insights of modern psychology to help him. But he did have the Hebrew Scriptures, pointing the way through the hard-won wisdom of sufferers like Job and the psalmists.

You have the same guidebook, enriched with the Gospel record of Jesus' life and teachings, as well as the other New Testament books, which reflect his followers' attempts to apply his teachings to their lives. As you struggle beneath the weight of your cross, look to the words Jesus read and spoke and inspired. In balance with the best of today's knowledge and wisdom, they will help you follow Jesus past Calvary to Easter joy.

JESUS WOULD...

Look for meaning, not reasons

Why? That word has risen from troubled hearts since the world began. It's not really a plea for explanations—in our scientific age, we can name more reasons for things that happen than any generation before us. We can name causes for disease; we can list the factors in an accident.

Rather, the *whys* we hurl to heaven are cries for meaning. Suffering turns the world upside-down and shakes all our certainties—perhaps even our faith. We seek meaning in order to recover our balance.

JESUS READ...

It isn't easy

For the reasoning of mortals is worthless, and our designs are likely to fail....We can hardly guess at what is on earth, and what is at hand we find with labor; but who has traced out what is in the heavens? Who has learned your counsel, unless you have given wisdom and sent your holy spirit from on high?

WISDOM 9:14, 16-17

JESUS WOULD...

Know that everyone suffers

"Why me?" you ask. It would make as much sense to ask, "Why not me?" For suffering is part and parcel of our world. Everything that lives must die; every creature feels pain at some time.

We humans are at a special disadvantage: we are thinking beings. We can hold past, present, and future in our minds all at once. We weep for what was and worry about what will be. Alone of all creatures, we resist pain and question our fate.

JESUS READ...

Life is hard

A mortal, born of woman, few of days and full of trouble, comes up like a flower and withers, flees like a shadow and does not last. For there is hope for a tree, if it is cut down, that it will sprout again, and that its shoots will not cease. But mortals die, and are laid low; humans expire, and where are they?

JOB 14:1-2, 7, 10

JESUS WOULD...

Refuse blame

We can't help thinking that what we suffer is somehow our fault, that we must have done something to deserve what we are going through. Over and over we ask ourselves what we did to earn such a punishment. We don't pretend to be perfect. But surely our sins are small and have been forgiven. For what is God punishing us so severely?

JESUS SAID...

Suffering isn't punishment

As he walked along, he saw a man blind from birth. His disciples asked him, "Rabbi, who sinned, this man or his parents, that he was born blind?" Jesus answered, "Neither this man nor his parents sinned; he was born blind so that God's works might be revealed in him."

JOHN 9:1-3

9

JESUS WOULD...

Allow grief

"Keep a stiff upper lip. Quit feeling sorry for yourself. Put it behind you and get on with life." This is the message we get at every turn—even possibly what we tell ourselves. Our society has little patience with suffering people.

But society is wrong. Just as a broken leg needs time and care before we can walk on it again, a broken heart needs time to grieve. Until we have mourned the loss of health or happiness, we cannot make peace with it.

JESUS DID...

Feel sorrow

When Mary came where Jesus was and saw him, she knelt at his feet and said to him, "Lord, if you had been here, my brother would not have died." When Jesus saw her weeping, and the Jews who came with her also weeping, he was greatly disturbed in spirit and deeply moved. He said, "Where have you laid him?" They said to him, "Lord, come and see." Jesus began to weep.

JOHN 11:32-35

JESUS WOULD...

Embrace brokenness

When life is good, we seem to need nothing more. God's love is just the icing on the cake, something we take for granted.

But when pain catches us in its claws, we begin to realize what frail creatures we are. We realize that we aren't self-sufficient at all, that life is not something under our control. We cry out to anyone who will listen. We cry out helplessly to God, and begin at last to grow in wisdom and real strength.

JESUS TAUGHT...

I give you strength

Three times I appealed to the Lord about this, that it would leave me, but he said to me, "My grace is sufficient for you, for power is made perfect in weakness." So, I will boast all the more gladly of my weaknesses, so that the power of Christ may dwell in me. Therefore I am content with weaknesses, insults, hardships, persecutions, and calamities for the sake of Christ; for whenever I am weak, then I am strong.

2 CORINTHIANS 12:8-10

JESUS WOULD...

Own the pain

We do not tolerate a headache for long without reaching for a pill. The pain you are now suffering is both greater and more constant. You naturally want to escape it. You try to pretend it isn't there. You may try to numb it by keeping very busy; drugs and alcohol promise brief relief. But nothing really works for very long.

Your pain is real—it's yours and you have every right to feel so bad. Don't try to wish away your suffering. Claim it!

JESUS SAID...

It hurts

They went to a place called Gethsemane; and he said to his disciples, "Sit here while I pray." He took with him Peter and James and John, and began to be distressed and agitated. And said to them, "I am deeply grieved, even to death; remain here, and keep awake." And going a little farther, he threw himself on the ground and prayed that, if it were possible, the hour might pass from him.

MARK 14:32-35

JESUS WOULD...

Accept the feelings

Fear, guilt, anger, regret, and depression weave in and through our days. We are not at all proud of some of the things we feel. We try to hide them even from ourselves. But feelings are neither good nor bad; they just are.

Accept as valid whatever you may be feeling. Your goodness lies in dealing with them as constructively as you can, not in trying to deny them or bury them out of reach. Face them squarely and work with them.

JESUS SAID...

I understand

"Come to me, all you that are weary and are carrying heavy burdens, and I will give you rest. Take my yoke upon you, and learn from me; for I am gentle and humble in heart, and you will find rest for your souls. For my yoke is easy, and my burden is light."

MATTHEW 11:28-30

17

JESUS WOULD...

Cry

Tears are a sign of weakness, they say. Not so! Tears are a way of coping, nature's remedy for hurt. Unshed tears make your head throb and increase the level of acid in your stomach. Crying helps to wash away pain and stress. Shedding tears even releases certain brain chemicals that are natural pain relievers.

So let the tears fall without shame or embarrassment. If crying makes others uncomfortable, allow yourself a good cry in private.

JESUS READ...

Tears have their place

For everything there is a season, and a time for every matter under heaven...a time to weep, and a time to laugh; a time to mourn, and a time to dance.

ECCLESIASTES 3:1, 4

JESUS WOULD...

Feel anger

You may feel angry at your situation, at the people who contributed to it, or at those who are not helpful or responsive to your needs. You may even be angry at God. And you are ashamed of your rage.

Anger can indeed lead to evil actions, but it can also be a sign of strength and caring. The trick is to direct it constructively. If you try to bury it, it will erupt in unmanageable ways. Learn to vent it without hurting anyone.

JESUS SAID...

Get angry

Again he entered the synagogue, and a man was there who had a withered hand. They watched him to see whether he would cure him on the sabbath, so that they might accuse him. And he said to the man who had the withered hand, "Come forward." Then he said to them, "Is it lawful to do good or to do harm on the sabbath, to save life or to kill?" But they were silent. He looked around at them with anger.

MARK 3:1-5

JESUS WOULD...

Express regrets

Had you seen this coming, you'd have acted differently. You would have kept a better health watch; you would not have started a quarrel.

You can torture yourself with "I should have...," or you can simply admit that you are not perfect. Acknowledge your regrets. Express them to anyone you may have injured. Express them to God. In the power we call prayer, you can even make peace with someone who is on the other side of the grave.

JESUS SAID...

I wish...

"Jerusalem, Jerusalem, the city that kills the prophets and stones those who are sent to it! How often have I desired to gather your children together as a hen gathers her brood under her wings, and you were not willing! See, your house is left to you, desolate."

MATTHEW 23:37-38

JESUS WOULD...

Tend relationships

Injured animals snap and snarl. So do hurting people. Unlike animals, people are most likely to lash out at the very folks who are closest to them. Who else, after all, can be expected to take it?

But these are the very people whose support you need most while you are suffering. However hard it is to be sensitive to someone's else's feelings when yours are so overpowering, tend these relationships with special care.

JESUS SAID...

First things first

"So when you are offering your gift at the altar, if you remember that your brother or sister has something against you, leave your gift there before the altar and go; first be reconciled to your brother or sister, and then come and offer your gift."

MATTHEW 5:23

JESUS WOULD...

Understand loneliness

No one knows how you feel. Sensitive people or those who have gone through similar suffering may come close, but no one else can ever fully understand what is going on inside you.

And many folks will feel helpless because they can't "fix" it for you. Unsure of what to say or do, even the persons you have always been able to count on may back off. Believe that they really do care—but look for people who are less afraid of your pain.

JESUS READ...

Suffering is a lonely business

My acquaintances are wholly estranged from me. My relatives and my close friends have failed me;...I have become an alien in their eyes....I am loathsome to my own family....All my intimate friends abhor me, and those whom I loved have turned against me.

JOB 19:13-15, 17, 19

JESUS WOULD...

Seek solitude

Sometimes the least lonely place to be is by yourself. There you can scream or cry; you can say whatever you feel out loud without getting blank stares. You can sit and write out your feelings; you can pace the floor. You can get fully in touch with your emotions and try to think through what you most need.

All those possibilities may be more than a little frightening. But you never need be really alone: God is near.

JESUS SAID...

Go off alone

In the morning, while it was still very dark, he got up and went out to a deserted place, and there he prayed. And Simon and his companions hunted for him. When they found him, they said to him, "Everyone is searching for you."

MARK 1:35-37

JESUS WOULD...

Pray alone

Whenever life got stressful, Jesus sought a quiet spot away from the crowd and had a heart-to-heart talk with his Father.

Follow his example: set aside some solitary time to address God. If prayer words won't come, settle for the bare minimum. "Help me!" or "Are you there?" is enough, if that's all you can manage. Or pour your heart out to God, if you like. In any case, know that God is always near, listening attentively to your need.

JESUS SAID...

Spend time alone with God

"But whenever you pray, go into your room and shut the door and pray to your Father who is in secret; and your Father who sees in secret will reward you."

MATTHEW 6:6

31

JESUS WOULD...

Listen carefully to the silence

God isn't very talkative. Chances are you won't hear a voice assuring you everything will be all right or telling you what you can do to ease the pain. But don't read God's silence as cold indifference. Think of the many times someone has spoken quiet volumes to you just by sending a smile across the room, sitting beside you, holding you.

God's silence is like that. Without a word, God speaks infinite love and compassion.

JESUS READ...

Hush!

"Be still, and know that I am God! I am exalted among the nations, I am exalted in the earth." The Lord of hosts is with us; the God of Jacob is our refuge.

PSALM 46:10

JESUS WOULD...

Turn to tradition

Jesus was brought up in the religious tradition of the Israelites. He continually looked to this tradition for its deepest meaning and let it nurture his sense of God's tenderness and compassion.

Draw on the riches of your faith tradition. Recall the words about suffering that really make sense to you. Call the fellow believer who seems blessed with inner strength and serenity. Talk with one of the people who minister to your community.

JESUS TAUGHT...

You have good company

Therefore, since we are surrounded by so great a cloud of witnesses, let us also lay aside every weight and the sin that clings so closely, and let us run with perseverance the race that is set before us, looking to Jesus the pioneer and perfecter of our faith, who for the sake of the joy that was set before him endured the cross, disregarding its shame, and has taken his seat at the right hand of the throne of God.

HEBREWS 12:1-2

Jesus Would...

Use Scripture as a mirror

Although our world is quite different from theirs, we all have much in common with the folks who appear in the Bible. They too faced difficulties; they too searched for meaning, for understanding of God's ways.

Search the Bible, especially the Gospels, for someone whose shoes fit you, and walk in them for a while. How do you think that person felt facing God or Jesus of Nazareth? Is there something you need to imitate?

JESUS SAID...

This is *my* story

He stood up to read, and the scroll of the prophet Isaiah was given to him. He...found the place where it was written: "The Spirit of the Lord is upon me, because he has anointed me to bring good news to the poor. He has sent me to proclaim release to the captives and recovery of sight to the blind, to let the oppressed go free...." Then he began to say to them, "Today this scripture has been fulfilled in your hearing."

LUKE 4:16-21

Jesus Would...

Rethink who God is

Many images of God appear in Scripture—images God's people drew from their experience. Jesus drew on memories of a happy, love-filled childhood for his favorite image of God: *Abba*, an intimate version of "Father."

Recall the people who have best reflected God's love in your life. Does your image of God resemble them? Is your God loving Father or Mother, Friend, Lover, Healer, Savior? These are strong biblical images; take comfort in them.

JESUS READ...

God is a tender parent

When Israel was a child, I loved him, and out of Egypt I called my son....I took them up in my arms; but they did not know that I healed them. I led them with cords of human kindness, with bands of love. I was to them like those who lift infants to their cheeks. I bent down to them and fed them.

HOSEA 11:1, 3-4

Jesus Would...

Remember God's goodness

Jesus' people remembered God's actions so vividly that they took part in their ancestors' experience through special rituals—just as Christians at Eucharist take part in the death and rising of Jesus.

On a more personal level, believers can recall God's blessings in their own lives. Consider the many ways God has blessed you—not only the great joys, but also the small delights like the taste of ice cream or the beauty of a sunset—and give thanks to your God.

JESUS READ...

God is faithful

Can a woman forget her nursing child, or show no compassion for the child of her womb? Even these may forget, yet I will not forget you. See, I have inscribed you on the palms of my hands.

ISAIAH 49:15-16

JESUS WOULD...

Reject religious platitudes

"There is a reason." "God has a plan." Great human struggles have shaped these faith statements. But when they come from people who have never struggled, they have a hollow sound.

Jesus resisted the common urge to reduce religion to simple formulas. He scolded the religious leaders who tried to turn faith into a list of rules, protesting that compassion was a greater value.

Put your trust in people who show care, not those who have answers.

JESUS SAID...

Get back to basics

When the Pharisees saw this, they said to his disciples, "Why does your teacher eat with tax collectors and sinners?" But when he heard this, he said, "Those who are well have no need of a physician, but those who are sick. Go and learn what this means, 'I desire mercy, not sacrifice.' For I have come to call not the righteous but sinners."

MATTHEW 9:11-13

43

JESUS WOULD...

Be honest with God

One misconception believers sometimes have is that prayer is talking nicely to God. "Accept God's will," they say. "Don't question; don't argue." Yet reluctance to express your darker feelings can cripple your ability to pray.

Speak your questions—even your anger—in your prayer. The One who made us knows what is in our hearts and is not easily shocked. The folks who were closest to God knew that. Jesus, like Abraham before him, prayed boldly.

JESUS READ...

Speak out

After these things the word of the Lord came to Abram in a vision, "Do not be afraid, Abram, I am your shield; your reward shall be very great." But Abram said, "O Lord God, what will you give me, for I continue childless, and the heir of my house is Eliezer of Damascus?" And Abram said, "You have given me no offspring, and so a slave born in my house is to be my heir."

GENESIS 15:1-3

45

Jesus Would...

Pray the psalms

The Book of Psalms is Israel's prayer book. Alone or in community, God's people prayed its words. And the Psalms are prayers so bluntly honest they shock modern readers. (Could you ask God to see the heads of your enemies' babies smashed? See Psalm 137:9.)

The book contains prayers of bitter lament as well as songs of praise, prayers that express near despair as well as hope—sometimes in the same breath. Pray the Psalms as Jesus did.

JESUS READ...

A mix of feelings

My God, my God, why have you forsaken me? Why are you so far from helping me, from the words of my groaning? O my God, I cry by day, but you do not answer; and by night, but find no rest. Yet you are holy, enthroned on the praises of Israel. In you our ancestors trusted; they trusted, and you delivered them.

PSALM 22:1-4

JESUS WOULD...

Wrestle with God in prayer

Jesus knew well the story of his ancestor Jacob, who wrestled all night with an angel—a common metaphor for God in the Hebrew Scriptures. Jacob was profoundly affected by his struggle. Ever after he walked with a limp—but he also walked in strong faith.

Perhaps Jesus thought of Jacob as he wrestled with God in the Garden of Gethsemane, and drew strength from the story. Certainly you can borrow some of Jacob's courage and find his faith.

JESUS READ...

Jacob's story

Then the man said, "You shall no longer be called Jacob, but Israel, for you have striven with God and with humans, and have prevailed." Then Jacob asked him, "Please tell me your name." But he said, "Why is it that you ask my name?" And there he blessed him. So Jacob called the place Peniel, saying, "For I have seen God face to face, and yet my life is preserved." The sun rose upon him as he passed Peniel, limping because of his hip.

GENESIS 32:28-31

JESUS WOULD...

Take comfort in ritual

Human beings are ritual-makers even when they are small. A tiny tot fends off monsters in the dark with familiar bedtime routines. Believers fend off the forces of darkness with worship rituals.

As the forces of darkness closed in around him, Jesus celebrated Israel's greatest ritual—the Passover meal—and changed it into the Supper his followers still celebrate today. Look to the rites of your faith tradition for comfort.

JESUS SAID...

We need rituals

He said to them, "I have eagerly desired to eat this Passover with you before I suffer; for I tell you, I will not eat it until it is fulfilled in the kingdom of God." Then he took a loaf of bread, and when he had given thanks, he broke it and gave it to them, saying, "This is my body, which is given for you. Do this in remembrance of me."

LUKE 22:15-16, 19

JESUS WOULD...

Seek understanding hearts

Many people followed Jesus, but he shared his heart with only a chosen twelve. Even they were slow to understand him, as the Gospels testify, and one eventually betrayed him.

It's no easier in our own time to find a dozen folks who can really hear us. Count yourself blessed if you can find two or three. But you won't find any if you don't take the risk of baring your heart to likely candidates. And finding even one is worth the risk.

JESUS READ...

Treasure good friends

Faithful friends are a sturdy shelter: whoever finds one has found a treasure. Faithful friends are beyond price; no amount can balance their worth. Faithful friends are life-saving medicine; and those who fear the Lord will find them.

SIRACH 6:14-16

Jesus Would...

Pray with others

Jesus was so familiar in his hometown synagogue that he was asked to read from the sacred scrolls of Scripture (see Luke 4:16-22). He went often to the Jerusalem temple, where he celebrated the great Jewish feasts. He prayed with his friends at the sabbath meal. And he asked them to pray with him on the eve of his death.

Ask your friends to pray with you. Try something simple like the Lord's Prayer if you feel uncomfortable at first.

JESUS SAID...

Pray together

"Again, truly I tell you, if two of you agree on earth about anything you ask, it will be done for you by my Father in heaven. For where two or three are gathered in my name, I am there among them."

MATTHEW 18:19-20

JESUS WOULD...

Trust the community

Jesus not only gave himself to us, he also gave us to each other. Those who suffer in mind or body always have a special place in the prayers of the people who gather in his name.

They also have a claim on those people's care. Your faith community is rich in resources: people who can visit, counsel you, or lend a hand with all kinds of practical matters. Freely ask and gladly accept whatever you need—and enable others to serve the Lord.

JESUS READ...

Seek good company

As much as you can, aim to know your neighbors, and consult with the wise. Let your conversation be with intelligent people and let all your discussion be about the law of the Most High. Let the righteous be your dinner companions, and let your glory be in the fear of the Lord.

SIRACH 9:14-16

JESUS WOULD...

Accept helplessness

You may have a long list of things you can't get done. Physical or mental suffering often erodes our ability to function as we used to, and we feel completely helpless.

It's hard to think of Jesus as helpless. The Gospels are filled with stories of his power to heal the sick and raise the dead, calm the stormy sea and feed the multitude. Yet his greatest healing action was to hang in helpless agony on a cross on Calvary.

JESUS SAID...

Let go and let God

"Look at the birds of the air; they neither sow nor reap nor gather into barns, and yet your heavenly Father feeds them. Are you not of more value than they? Consider the lilies of the field, how they grow; they neither toil nor spin, yet I tell you, even Solomon in all his glory was not clothed like one of these."

MATTHEW 6:26, 28

JESUS WOULD...

Let God be God

From time immemorial, people have searched for a prayer that "works"—a prayer with an iron-clad guarantee. But any prayer that seeks to force God to obey us seeks to reverse the roles of creatures and Creator.

We are not in control of the universe, but neither is it spinning out of control. Allow the God who set it in motion to continue lovingly to tend to its workings.

JESUS SAID...

You're not in charge here

"When you are praying, do not heap up empty phrases as the Gentiles do; for they think that they will be heard because of their many words. Do not be like them, for your Father knows what you need before you ask him."

MATTHEW 6:7-8

JESUS WOULD...

Name the need

What do you need most urgently? What will it take right now to help you make it through this day?

Consider that question daily, and make it the focus of your prayer. Pray, too, that God will help you see the answer that lies right within your reach. It may be as near as your telephone, as simple as placing a request before a friend or acquaintance. It may even lie within your own heart.

JESUS SAID...

God understands your need

"Therefore do not worry....For it is the Gentiles who strive for all these things; and indeed your heavenly Father knows that you need all these things. But strive first for the kingdom of God and his righteousness, and all these things will be given to you as well. So do not worry about tomorrow, for tomorrow will bring worries of its own. Today's trouble is enough for today."

MATTHEW 6:31-34

JESUS WOULD...

Remember the promises

Israel's most inspiring Scripture was written in the nation's darkest days. The prophets sang their loveliest songs of God's care to a people who had been conquered and marched into exile far from home, leaving their land in ruins behind them.

Imagine how their promises must have sounded to people laboring in slavery in Babylon, how hard they must have wanted to believe them. And recall that God never forgets a promise.

JESUS READ...

God has plans for us

For I am about to create new heavens and a new earth; the former things shall not be remembered or come to mind. But be glad and rejoice forever in what I am creating; for I am about to create Jerusalem as a joy, and its people as a delight. I will rejoice in Jerusalem, and delight in my people; no more shall the sound of weeping be heard in it, or the cry of distress.

ISAIAH 65:17-19

JESUS WOULD...

Seek God's will

Everything happens for a reason, so they say. One pretty image suggests that God is weaving a beautiful tapestry out of the events of our lives, but that we can only see the knots and tangles of the underside. But truly skillful hands create beauty on both sides. A better understanding is that God can bring good out of any evil. The best understanding is that God intends only good, only beauty for all of creation.

God's will be done!

Jesus Read...

God wills good things

God did not make death, and he does not delight in the death of the living. For he created all things so that they might exist; the generative forces of the world are wholesome, and there is no destructive poison in them, and the dominion of Hades is not on earth.

WISDOM 1:13-14

JESUS WOULD...

Pray persistently

What's the use of praying when no one seems to be listening?

Yet prayer is not just a means of getting something; it is also an admission of your dependence on a loving God. Like any conversation between people who love each other, prayer deepens a relationship. People who stop talking to each other from the heart grow apart.

Keep talking. God does listen.

JESUS SAID...

Don't give up

"Ask, and it will be given you; search, and you will find; knock, and the door will be opened for you. For everyone who asks receives, and everyone who searches finds, and for everyone who knocks, the door will be opened. Is there anyone among you who, if your child asks for bread, will give a stone?...If you then...know how to give good gifts to your children, how much more will your Father in heaven give good things to those who ask him!"

MATTHEW 7:7-9, 11

69

JESUS WOULD...

Be patient

"Lord give me patience—right now!" That old joke probably finds an echo in your prayer. You want what the pain-reliever ads promise: instant relief.

Welcome to the human race! Surely Jesus did, too. But he clung to the belief that something wonderful was afoot in the world: the slow unfolding of God's kingdom.

Search your memory for God's activity in your life. Look around you for the signs that the kingdom is unfolding in your life, in your neighborhood, in the world.

JESUS SAID...

Good things are happening!

"The kingdom of God is as if someone would scatter seed on the ground, and would sleep and rise night and day, and the seed would sprout and grow, he does not know how. The earth produces of itself, first the stalk, then the head, then the full grain in the head."

MARK 4:26-28

JESUS WOULD...

Be sensitive to others' pain

It's hard to care about what someone else is going through when you're in pain. It's hard even to notice that another person is troubled.

Yet other people also grow short-tempered or distracted when they are hurting. Look beyond the symptoms with a warm remark or a sensitive question and you may discover a companion on the road of human suffering. Offer to others the same understanding you yourself long to find.

Jesus Said...

I hear you

One of the criminals who were hanged there kept deriding him and saying, "Are you not the Messiah? Save yourself and us!"... Then [the other] said, "Jesus, remember me when you come into your kingdom." He replied, "Truly I tell you, today you will be with me in Paradise."

LUKE 23:39, 42-43

73

JESUS WOULD...

Identify with other sufferers

Like every other human, Jesus knew pain and fear. He knew not only the agony of Calvary; he also suffered misunderstanding and rejection even from his closest friends—not to mention such irritations as the common cold and aching feet. Yet his pain only intensified his solidarity with the whole human race.

Join him in prayer and concern for all who suffer.

JESUS TAUGHT...

I'm in this with you

Though he was in the form of God, [Jesus] did not regard equality with God as something to be exploited, but emptied himself, taking the form of a slave, being born in human likeness. And being found in human form, he humbled himself and became obedient to the point of death—even death on a cross.

PHILIPPIANS 2:6-8

JESUS WOULD...

Reach out to others

The best parts of yourself are probably formed from scar tissue. You respond most quickly when someone is going through a bad experience you have known yourself; you know the value of small gestures of kindness because you have taken comfort from such acts.

Keep in touch with that best part of you. However bad you feel, you can still make a phone call or write a letter. Offer some word of comfort or encouragement to a person who needs it.

JESUS SAID...

Help me!

"Then the righteous will answer him, 'Lord, when was it that we saw you hungry and gave you food, or thirsty and gave you something to drink? And when was it that we saw you a stranger and welcomed you, or naked and gave you clothing? And when was it that we saw you sick or in prison and visited you?' And the king will answer them, 'Truly I tell you, just as you did it to one of the least of these who are members of my family, you did it to me.'"

MATTHEW 25:37-40

JESUS WOULD...

Surrender in trust

Researchers placed crawling babies on a tabletop. Their mothers called to them from the other end, and the babies moved toward them. Suddenly the tabletop appeared to end; wood was replaced with glass. Instinctively afraid of falling, the babies stopped and looked to their mothers, checking the expression on their faces to see if it was safe to go on.

From the cross, Jesus looked to his Father—and took a leap of trust into the darkness.

JESUS SAID...

I'm in good hands

It was now about noon, and darkness came over the whole land until three in the afternoon, while the sun's light failed; and the curtain of the temple was torn in two. Then Jesus, crying with a loud voice, said, "Father, into your hands I commend my spirit." Having said this, he breathed his last.

LUKE 23:44-46

JESUS WOULD...

Expect good things

Jesus spoke of his coming death and resurrection in the Gospels. But whatever he believed God would do, the details must have been unclear if he was, as we claim, fully human. It surely must have been impossible for him, blinded by the blood flowing from his wounded head, to see ahead to Easter morning.

Yet even from the cross he clung to the vision, promising that the thief who hung beside him would see paradise with him that very day.

JESUS TAUGHT...

You'll be so surprised!

But, as it is written, "What no eye has seen, nor ear heard, nor the human heart conceived, what God has prepared for those who love him"—these things God has revealed to us through the Spirit; for the Spirit searches everything, even the depths of God.

1 CORINTHIANS 2:9-10

JESUS WOULD...

Refuse to accept defeat

Suffering is like being lost in a maze. Everywhere you turn, you come to another dead end. But somewhere there is an opening, and you won't find it if you give up and sit down. The only way out is to keep going, even when you walk blindly.

Take one day at a time—and treasure the good ones. As one dying person observed, "There still are good days." And there will be more. Even for Jesus, Easter morning lay on the other side of Good Friday.

JESUS READ...

Good will come of this

Surely he has borne our infirmities and carried our diseases; yet we accounted him stricken, struck down by God, and afflicted. But he was wounded for our transgressions, crushed for our iniquities; upon him was the punishment that made us whole, and by his bruises we are healed.

ISAIAH 53:4-4

WWJD Books
from One Caring Place

What Would Jesus Do...to Rise Above Stress?
What Would Jesus Do...to Live Anew After Loss?
What Would Jesus Do...to Live in Love Each Day?
What Would Jesus Do...to Find Meaning in Suffering?

Available at your favorite gift shop, bookstore,
or directly from:

One Caring Place
Abbey Press Publications
St. Meinrad, IN 47577
1-800-325-2511